Get Up and Go!

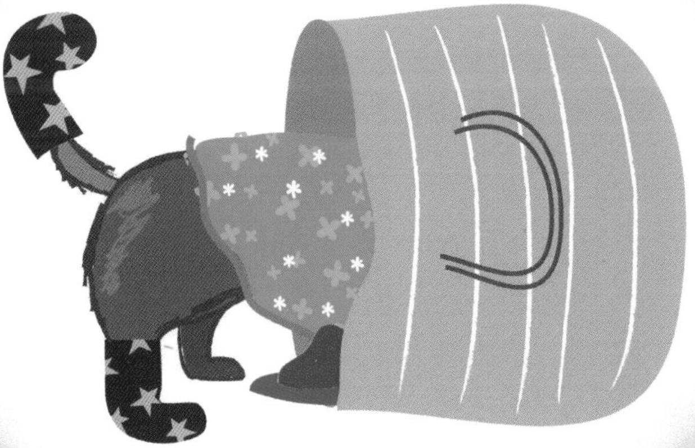

Written by Sheryl Webster
Illustrated by Sophie Webber

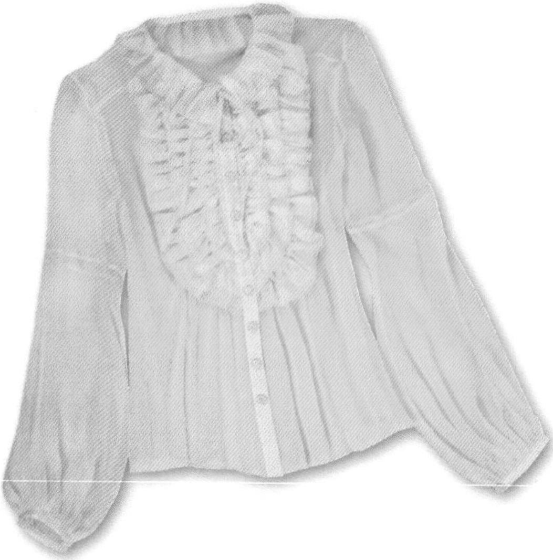

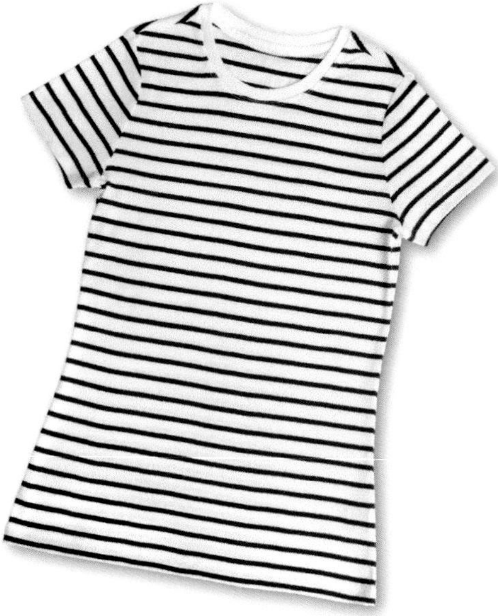

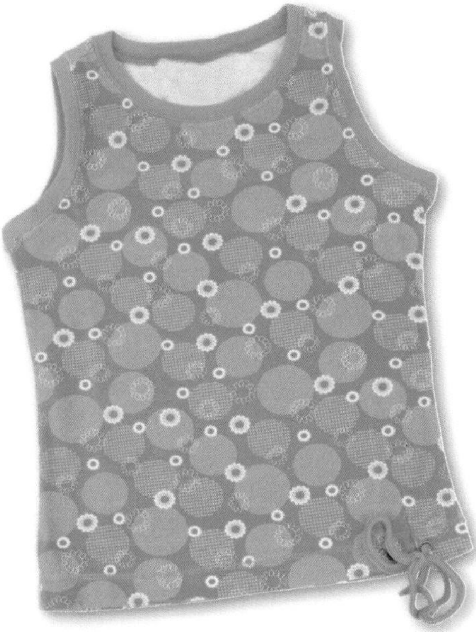

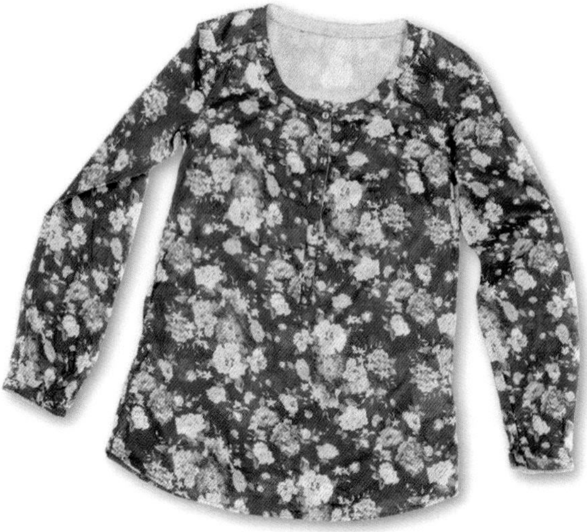

I get a top.

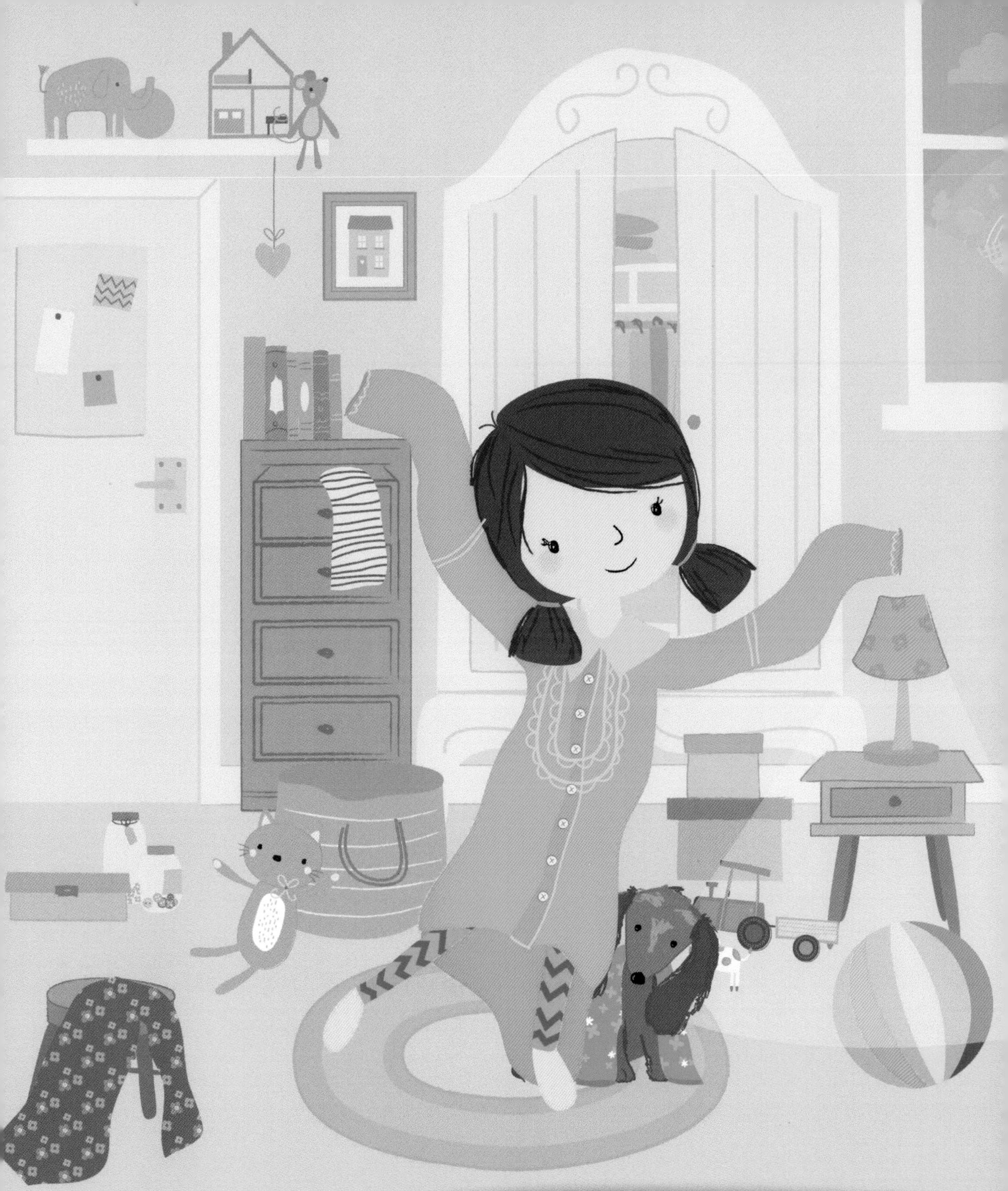

I put it on.

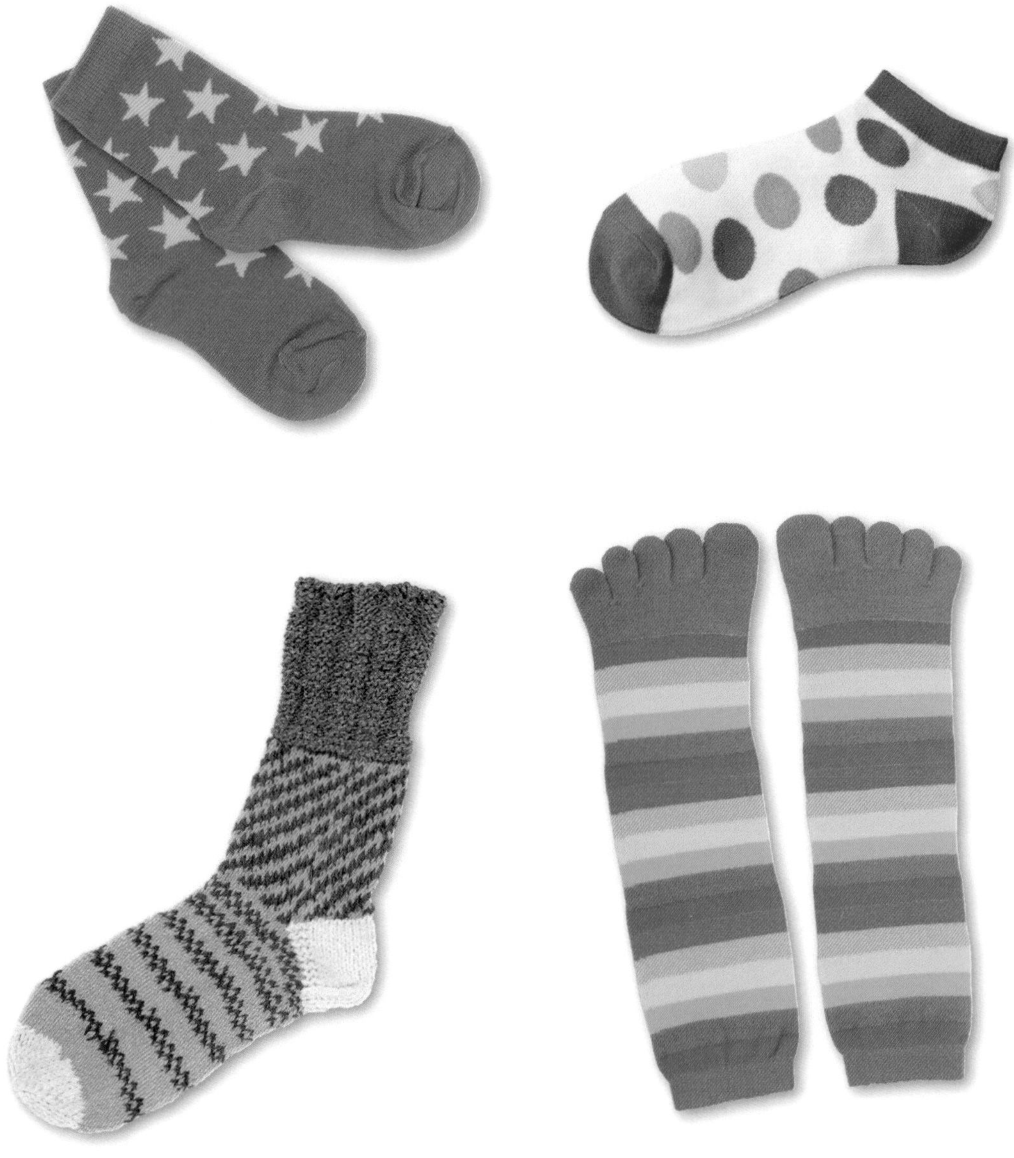

I get a sock.

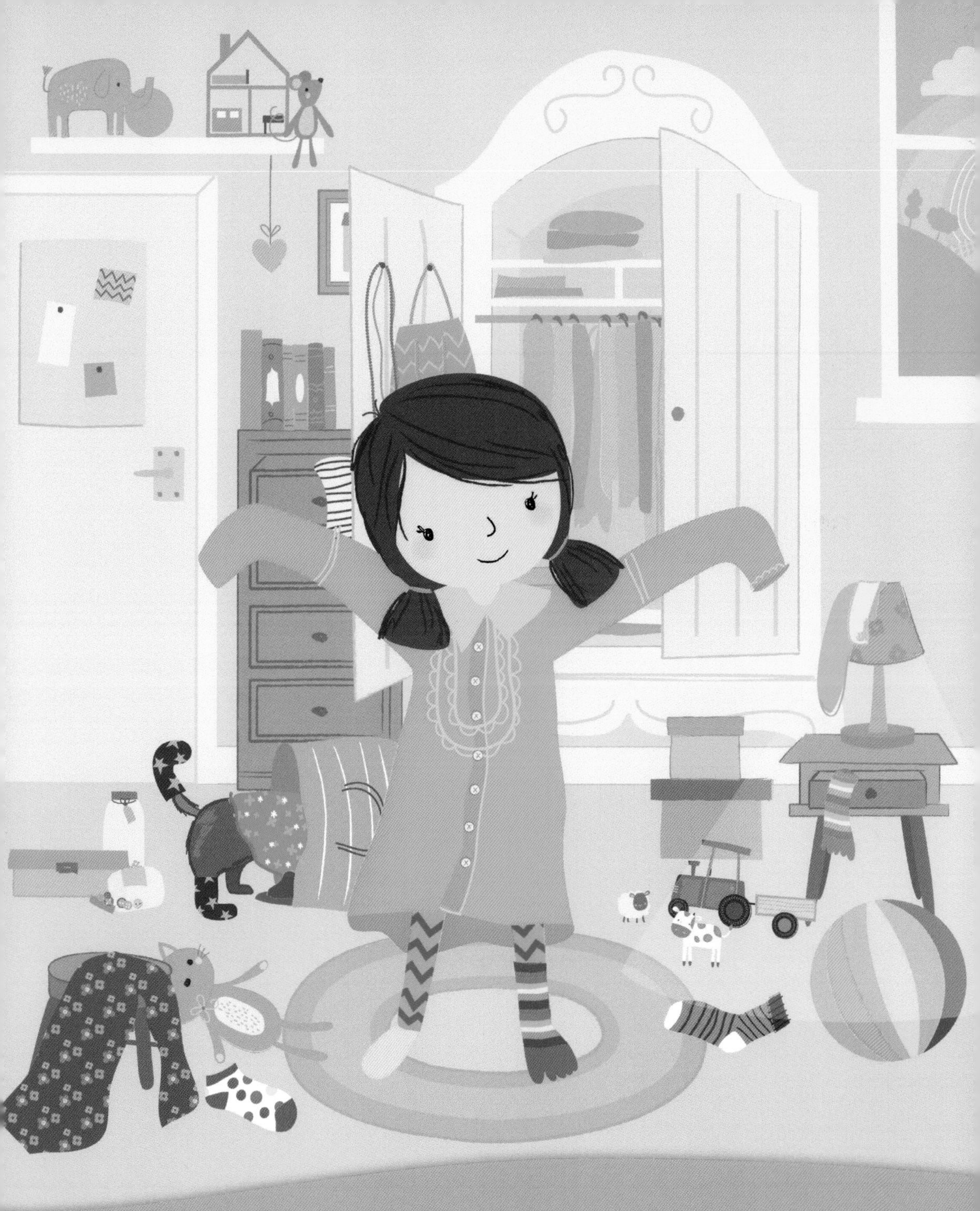

I put it on.

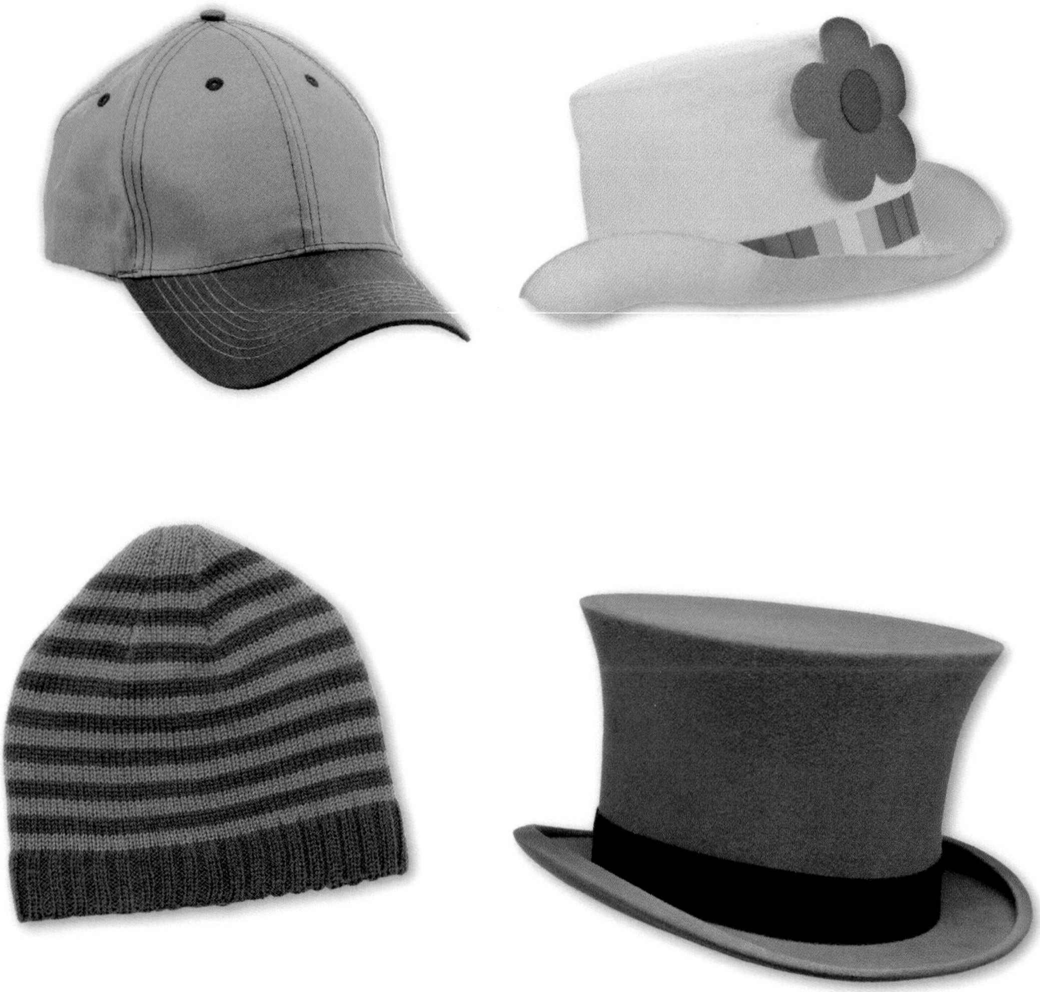

I get a cap.

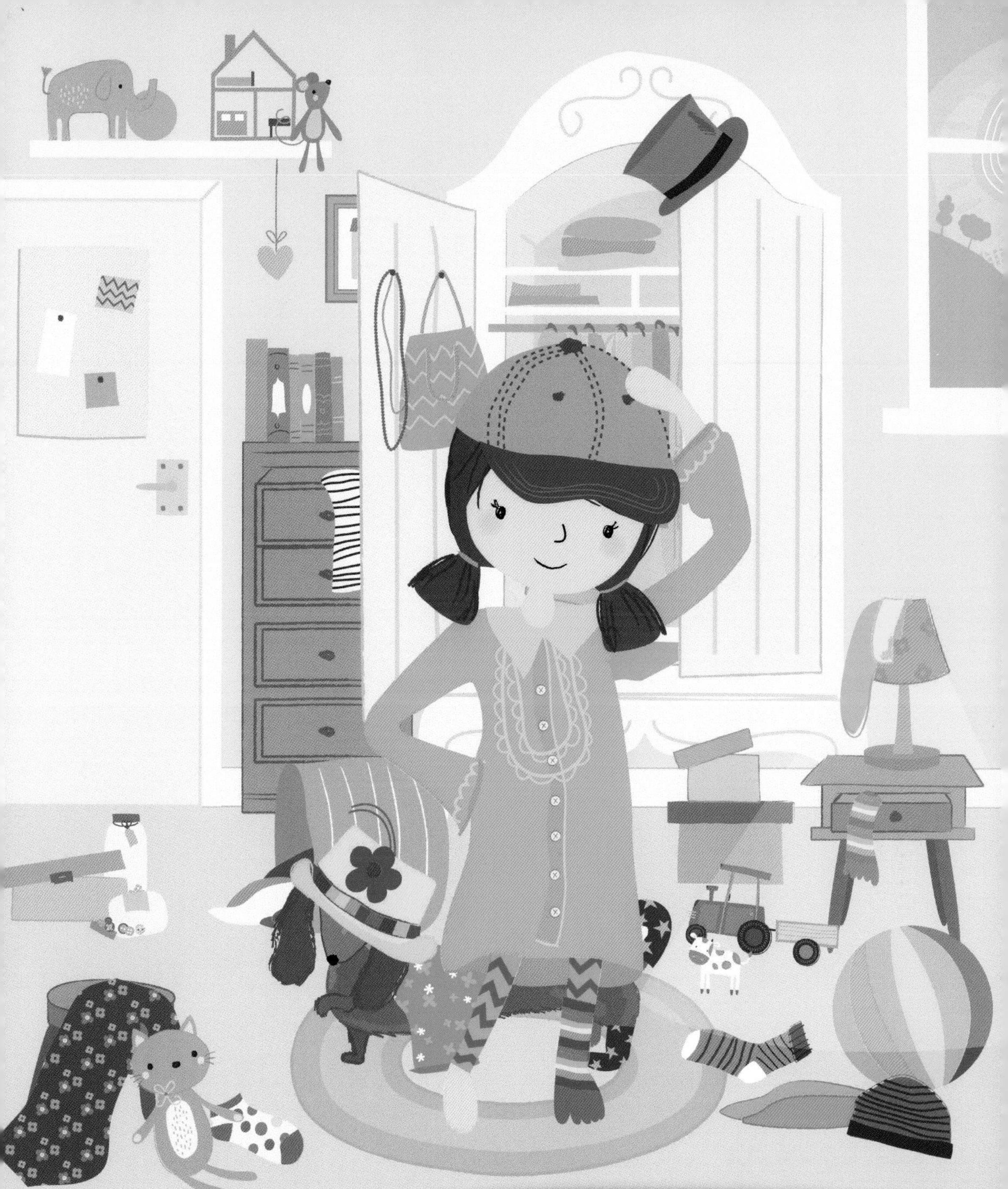

I put it on.

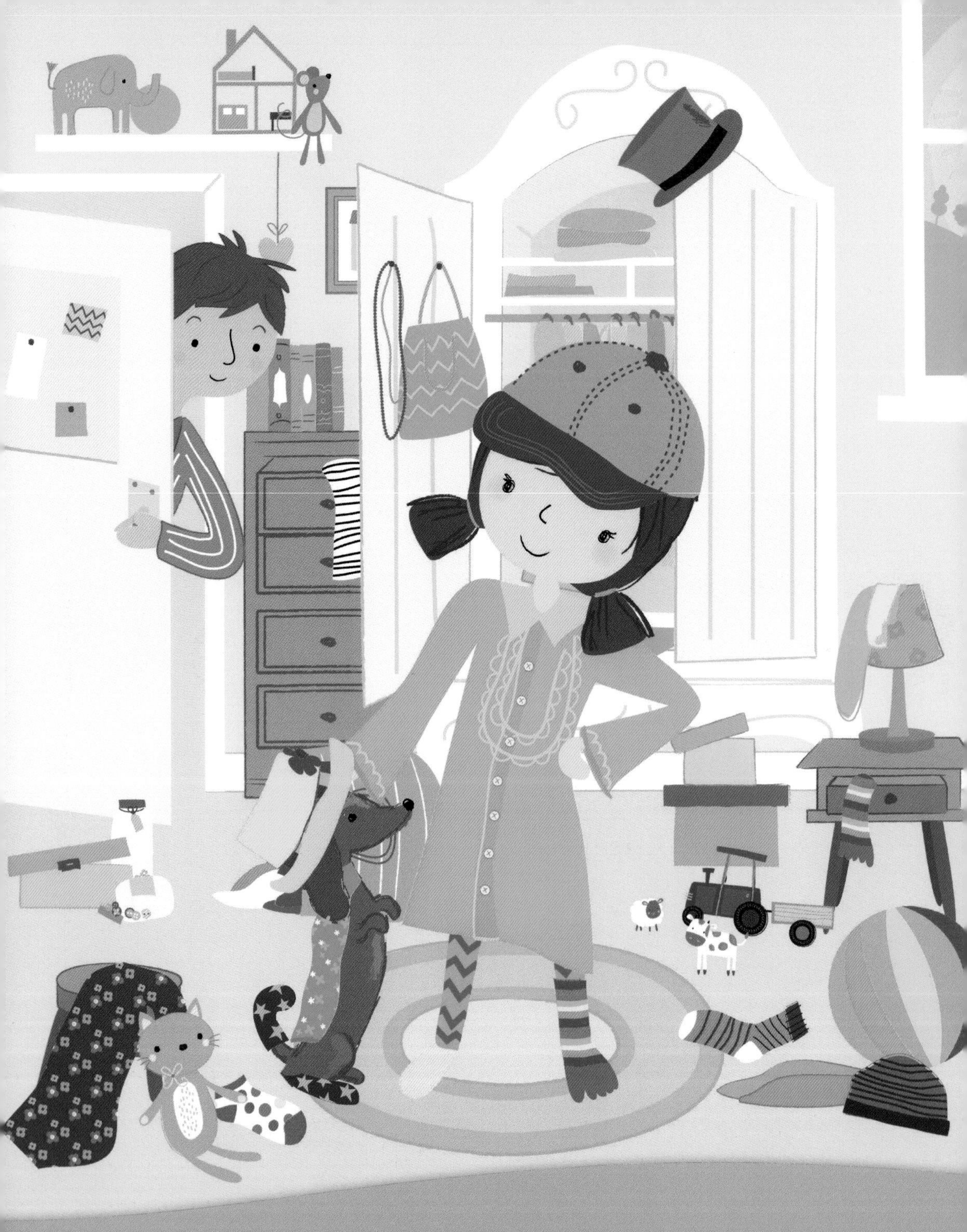

I get up and go!